W9-BKE-909

THE
LIBRARY OF BATS™

FREE-TAILED BATS

EMILY RAABE

The Rosen Publishing Group's
PowerKids Press™
New York

For Larry

Published in 2003 by The Rosen Publishing Group, Inc.
29 East 21st Street, New York, NY 10010

First Edition

Editor: Natashya Wilson
Book Design: Emily Muschinske

Photo Credits: Cover and title page, pp. 4, 5 (right) © ANT Photo Library; pp. 5 (top left), 6, 9, 11, 12, 16, 17, 18, 19, 21 © Robert and Linda Mitchell; p. 5 (map) Eric DePalo; pp. 7, 15 © Merlin D. Tuttle, Bat Conservation International; pp. 10, 15 (inset) © Roger W. Barbour/National Museum of Natural History/Smithsonian Institution; p. 13 © Michael Durham; p. 22 © David Liebman.

Raabe, Emily.
    Free-tailed bats / Emily Raabe. — 1st ed.
        p. cm. — (The library of bats)
    Includes bibliographical references (p.   ).
    Summary: An introduction to the appearance, behavior, and habitat of free-tailed bats, a large family of bats whose tails stick out beyond the flying membrane that makes up a bat's wings.
    ISBN 0-8239-6325-X (lib. bdg.)
    1. Free-tailed bats—Juvenile literature.   [1. Free-tailed bats. 2. Bats.]   I. Title. II. Series: Raabe, Emily. Library of bats
QL737.C54R224 2003
599.4'7—dc21

                2001006652

Manufactured in the United States of America

CONTENTS

THE FREE-TAILED BATS

There are nearly 1,000 different kinds of bats in the world. They are placed in 17 groups, called **families**. The free-tailed bat family is a large family of bats. There are 86 different kinds, or **species**, of bats in the free-tailed bat family. All free-tailed bats have what is called a free tail. This means that their tails stick out past their **flying membranes**. The flying membrane is the skin that makes up a bat's wings. Flying membranes stretch between bats' fingers to their shoulders, legs, and bodies. In many bats, this membrane also stretches between their two back legs. Many other bats' tails are covered by this membrane, but free-tailed bats' tails stick out.

Free-tailed bats' tails stick out past their flying membranes (left), as shown by a mastiff bat (top right). The map (bottom) shows where free-tailed bats live throughout the world.

BAT FACT

You can sometimes tell which family a bat belongs to by looking at its nose or its tail. Hog-nosed bats, for example, all have noses that look something like pigs' snouts. Plain-nosed bats all have plain noses. Leaf-nosed bats have folds of skin on their noses. Mouse-tailed bats have long, skinny tails, as do mice.

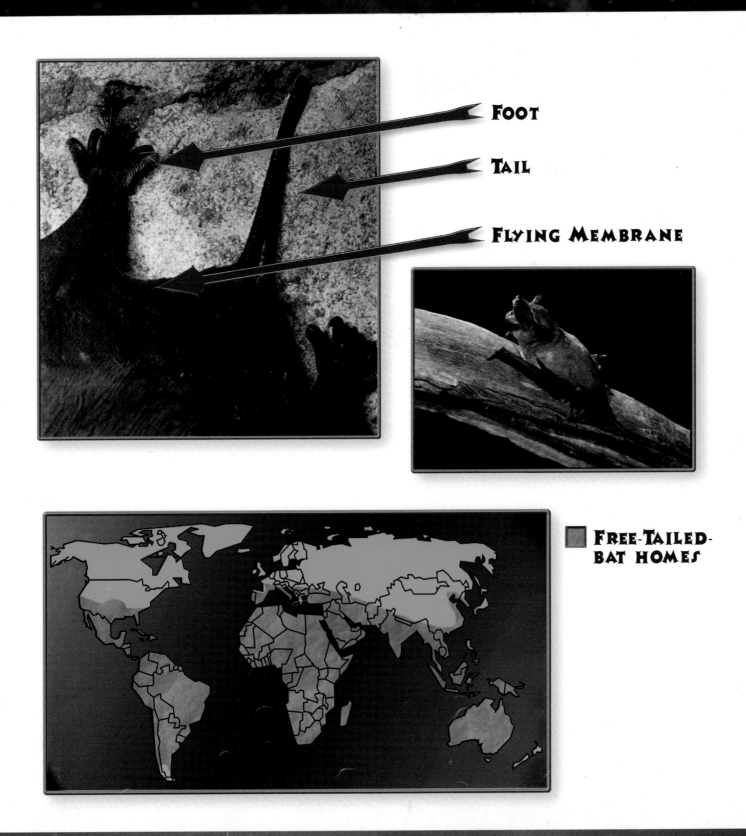

FOOT

TAIL

FLYING MEMBRANE

FREE-TAILED-
BAT HOMES

A Face Only a Bat Could Love

If you were to see a free-tailed bat, you might think it a little bit odd looking. Most free-tailed bats have thick, tough ears that are joined across their foreheads or on top of their heads, like a headband. Many free-tailed bats also have wrinkled upper lips. Free-tailed bats all have short, strong legs. They also have wide feet and thick, free tails. Free-tailed bats may not be pretty, but they are very good fliers. Their long, narrow wings are shaped for flying fast. These tough, leathery wings are also very strong. This means that free-tailed bats can fly for long periods of time without resting.

This Mexican free-tailed bat has wrinkly lips. Free-tailed bats are brown, black, gray, or tan, with short, velvety fur. They brush their fur with their feet to keep it neat.

Bat Fact

The smallest type of free-tailed bat in the United States is the Mexican free-tailed bat. This tiny bat weighs only ½ ounce (14 g). The largest free-tailed bat in the United States is the western mastiff bat *(above)*. This bat weighs approximately 2.0 to 2.5 ounces (65 g) and has a 21-inch (550-mm) wingspan.

WARM WEATHER BATS

Like most bats, free-tailed bats like hot weather. This is because most bats eat insects, which are plentiful in warm places. It is also because most bats do not have a lot of fur and would freeze to death in very cold weather. Africa and South America have the most species of free-tailed bats. Free-tailed bats also live in southern Europe and in southern Asia. In the United States, free-tailed bats live in the central and the southern states. Free-tailed bats **roost** in caves, in cracks in rocks, in buildings, and in hollow trees. Bats that live in cold parts of the world survive winters by **hibernating**, or sleeping all winter. Because they live in hot areas, free-tailed bats do not need to hibernate. However, some of them **migrate** to even warmer places in the winter.

BAT STATS

Free-tailed bats like their homes to be at least 110°F (43°C). Many free-tailed bats like to roost underneath tin roofs, because the tin gets very warm in the sun.

Mexican free-tailed bats snuggle together in their cave roost.

FLYING HIGH, FLYING FAR

Unlike other bats, free-tailed bats fly all night. They can fly as high as 10,000 feet (3,048 m) in the sky! Sometimes they fly six or seven hours without stopping to rest. They will travel as far as 31 miles (50 km) in one night to find food. Free-tailed bats eat moths and insects with hard shells, such as beetles and stinkbugs. To find their **prey** in the dark, they use something called **echolocation**. This means they send out a sound in front of themselves while they are flying. When the sound bounces off an object, the bats can tell how far away the object is by how long it takes the echo to come back to them.

Free-tailed bats usually leave their roosts later in the evening than do most bats.

BAT FACT

Western mastiff bats have smooth lips that help them to eat only certain parts of the insects they catch. By moving insects around with their talented lips, they can bite off the head, the wings, and the middle part of an insect and eat only the last body segment, called the abdomen.

Unusual Free-Tailed Bats

The free-tailed family has some unusual members. Sometimes a Mexican free-tailed bat will be born totally white! This all-white fur color is called **albino**. Some free-tailed bats have no fur at all. These naked bats live in the Philippines, on the island of Java, and in Borneo. They are hairless except for a few tiny hairs on their heads and bellies. Naked bats can tuck their wings into skin pouches on their bodies to crawl on the ground. Three types of free-tailed bats in Africa and in South America live under rocks. They have flattened heads to fit under the rocks and tough growths of skin on their arms to protect them from getting scraped.

Bat Fact

Naked bats are the only bats that tuck their wings into pouches in their skin, but other bats also do neat things with their wings. If it is hot, flying foxes *(above)* and fruit bats might lower one wing and flap it like a fan to cool off. Western big-eared bats roll up their enormous ears and cover themselves with their wings while they sleep.

It is easy to spot an albino Mexican free-tailed bat among its dark brown family members.

A Large Bat in the West

The western mastiff bat is the largest bat in the United States. This brown bat is usually from 6 to 7 inches (150–180 mm) long. Its wingspan is about 21 inches (550 mm). Western mastiff bats live in the American Southwest, northern Mexico, and South America. They roost under roofs, or in holes in the sides of cliffs. If you are ever walking in the southwestern United States on a summer evening, listen carefully. You might hear a strange peeping noise coming from the sky. That noise is the echolocation call of the western mastiff bat! Humans cannot hear most bats' echolocation calls. The western mastiff bat's call is one of the few that humans can hear.

Bat Stats

Western mastiff bats are so big that they cannot take off from the ground. They need to start from at least 15 feet (4.5 m) off the ground. From this height, a western mastiff bat drops into the air and begins to fly.

Inset: *Female western mastiff bats usually have one baby each year.*

Left: *Western mastiff bats have soft, velvety fur. Their large ears are connected across their foreheads.*

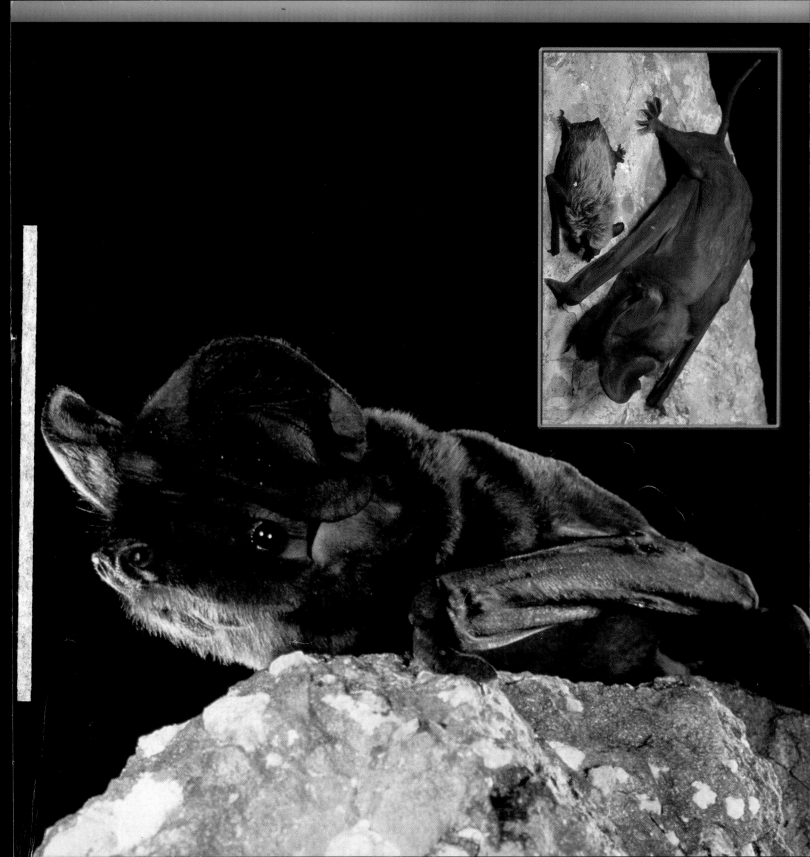

THE MEXICAN FREE-TAILED BAT

Mexican free-tailed bats are the smallest free-tailed bats. They are about the size of a human adult's thumb and weigh about ½ ounce (14 g). They live in the southern United States, in Central America, and in South America. Eagle Creek Cave in Arizona used to house from 25 to 50 million Mexican free-tailed bats! This was the world's largest **population** of free-tailed bats. By the late 1960s, the cave's bat population had dropped to about 30,000. One of the reasons for this was a chemical called **DDT**, which was used to kill insects. DDT also killed the animals that ate the insects, such as bats. It was banned in the United States in 1972.

Twenty million Mexican free-tailed bats live in Bracken Cave, near San Antonio, Texas.

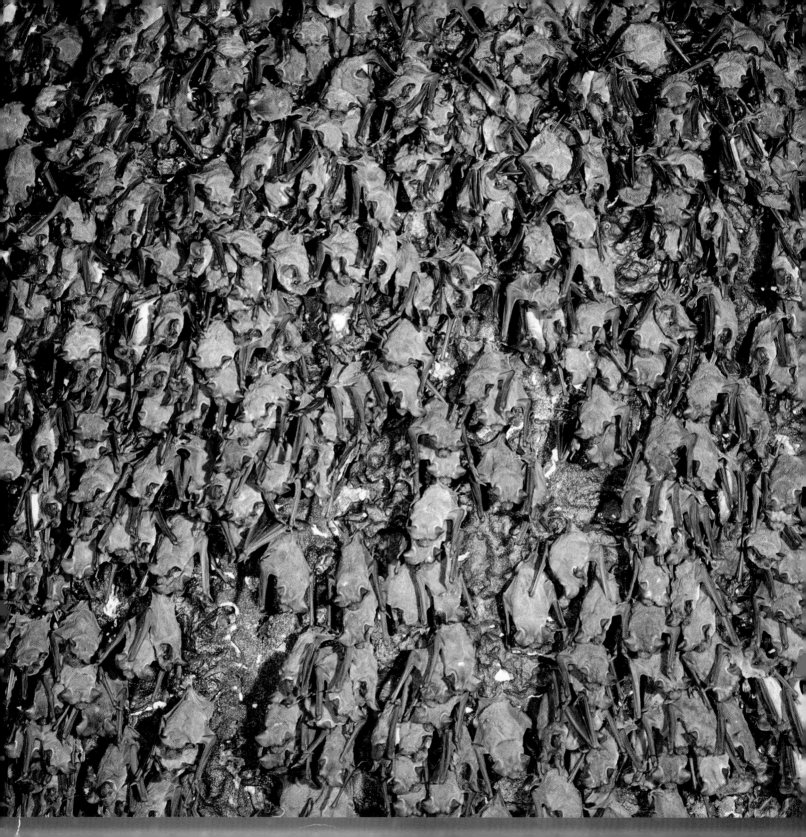

BABIES, BABIES, EVERYWHERE!

Female Mexican free-tailed bats and their babies in the southwestern United States live in summer roosts together. Baby bats are stuffed into these caves. There can be 500 baby bats per square foot (4,500 per sq m) in a **nursery** cave! How do mother bats find their own babies in such a crowd? For years scientists thought that mother Mexican free-tailed bats nursed any baby that lived in the nursery. Studies showed that almost all the mother bats fed only their own babies. Mother Mexican free-tailed bats are able to pick their own babies' smells and voices out of those of every other baby in the cave!

BAT FACT

In the summer, male Mexican free-tailed bats roost separately from the mothers and the babies in groups of from 10 to 300 bats. Many of the males live in Mexico all year. The females and the babies fly from the American Southwest to Mexico to join the males for the winter. In the winter, the male and female bats all roost together.

These hairless baby bats are part of a large nursery cave in Bracken Cave, Texas. Baby bats will try to beg milk from any female bat in the cave, but usually they have to wait for their own mothers to feed them.

Famous Bat Caves

Carlsbad Caverns in New Mexico is a well-known roost for Mexican free-tailed bats. In 1836, there were 8.7 million Mexican free-tailed bats in this cave. By 1973, this number had dropped to 200,000. Like the bats in Eagle Creek Cave, many bats in Carlsbad Caverns died from eating insects that had been sprayed with DDT. Many more bats were killed by people who either disturbed them accidentally or who wanted to kill them. Today the largest **colony** of **mammals** in the world lives in Bracken Cave in Texas. Twenty million female Mexican free-tailed bats live in this cave. When they have their babies in the spring and early summer, the population in the cave can grow to 40 million bats! Today Bracken Cave is protected with special gates that let bats in but that keep people out.

Bat Stats

Bracken Cave is home to the largest colony of mammals on Earth. Every night, these free-tailed bats eat up to 220,500 pounds (100,017 kg) of insects!

Bats darken the sky during their evening flight from Bracken Cave.

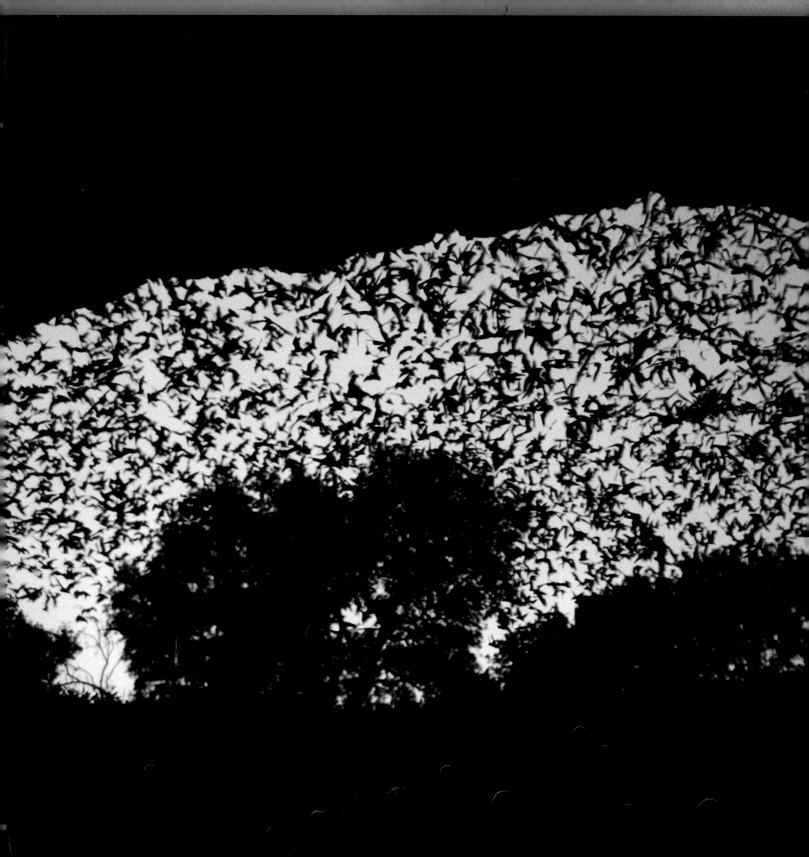

FREE-TAILED BATS AND PEOPLE

Free-tailed bats make good neighbors. The Mexican free-tailed bats in Bracken Cave help to control the insect population. Western mastiff bats eat moths that would otherwise eat farmers' crops. Naked bats eat pest insects, such as termites. People have not always been such good neighbors to bats, but today bats are being protected. In California, farmers build bat houses in their fields to attract free-tailed bats and other kinds of bats. They know that more bats mean fewer insects to harm their crops. In many countries in Europe, it is now against the law to harm bats. People all around the world are beginning to understand that bats just might make the best neighbors of all!

BAT FACT

Austin, Texas, is a town that loves its bats. Its Congress Avenue Bridge (above) is home to 1.5 million Mexican free-tailed bats. People gather near the bridge each night to watch the bats take flight. When new bridges are built in Austin, the builders make spaces under them for bat roosts. Austin's hockey team is named the Ice Bats!

GLOSSARY

albino (al-BY-noh) Pink-skinned with all-white fur.

colony (KAH-luh-nee) A group of people or animals living together.

DDT (DEE DEE TEE) A chemical that was sprayed on crops to kill insects.

echolocation (eh-koh-loh-KAY-shun) A method of locating objects by producing a sound and judging the time it takes the echo to return and the direction from which it returns. Bats, dolphins, porpoises, killer whales, and some shrews all use echolocation.

families (FAM-leez) Scientific groupings of plants and animals that are alike in some ways.

flying membranes (FLY-ing MEM-braynz) The skin that stretches between bats' fingers and shoulders and between their feet and tails, to make their wings.

hibernating (HY-bur-nayt-ing) Spending the winter in a sleeplike state, with heart rate and breathing slowed down.

mammals (MA-mulz) Animals that have hair and backbones and that feed their babies milk.

migrate (MY-grayt) To travel to find food or to escape cold weather.

nursery (NURS-ree) A place where babies are cared for.

population (pah-pyoo-LAY-shun) The number of any one kind of creature living in a place.

prey (PRAY) An animal that is hunted by another animal for food.

roost (ROOST) A place where bats or birds rest or sleep.

species (SPEE-sheez) A single kind of living thing. All humans are one species.

Index

Web Sites

To learn more about free-tailed bats, check out these Web sites:

www.batcon.org/batsmag/v10n3-1.html
www.museumca.org/caves/onli_echo_mastiff.html
www.thewildones.org/Animals/mexFree.html